# Independence Day

Mir Tamim Ansary

Heinemann Library
Chicago, Illinois

© 2002 Reed Educational & Professional Publishing
Published by Heinemann Library,
an imprint of Reed Educational & Professional Publishing,
Chicago, Illinois

Customer Service  888-454-2279
Visit our website at www.heinemannlibrary.com

Designed by Depke Design
Printed and bound at Lake Book Manufacturing

06 05 04 03 02
10 9 8 7 6 5 4 3 2 1

**Library of Congress Cataloging-in-Publication Data**
Ansary, Mir Tamim.
 Independence Day / Mir Tamim Ansary.
    p. cm. -- (Holiday histories)
Includes bibliographical references and index.
  ISBN 1-58810-223-8
  1.  Fourth of July--Juvenile literature. 2.  Fourth of July
celebrations--Juvenile literature. 3.  United States--History--Colonial
period, ca. 1600-1775--Juvenile literature. 4.  United
States--History--Revolution, 1775-1783--Juvenile literature. [1. Fourth
of July. 2. Holidays. 3. United States--History--Colonial period, ca.
1600-1775. 4. United States--History--Revolution, 1775-1783.] I. Title.

  E286 .A1246 2001
  394.2634--dc21

                                    2001000073

**Acknowledgments**
The author and publishers are grateful to the following for permission to reproduce
copyright material:
Cover photograph: Corbis
pp. 4–5 Gary A. Conner/Photo Edit; pp. 6–7 Jeff Greenberg/Photo Edit; p. 8 Culver Pictures; pp. 10,
13, 15, 20, 21, 25 The Granger Collection; pp. 11, 12, 16, 17, 18, 19, 22, 23, 26, 27 North Wind
Pictures; p. 14 Super Stock; p. 24 AP/Wide World; pp. 28–29 Deborah Davis/Photo Edit.

Every effort has been made to contact copyright holders of any material reproduced in this book.
Any omissions will be rectified in subsequent printings if notice is given to the publisher.

Some words are shown in bold, **like this.** You can find
out what they mean by looking in the glossary.

# Contents

# A Summer Holiday

**Independence** Day is our biggest summer holiday. It is always on the fourth of July. At this time of year, the days are long and warm.

4

Many families spend the holiday outdoors.
They watch parades. They go on picnics.
Then, as night falls, excitement grows.
Everyone knows what is coming—fireworks!

# Celebrating Our Independence

Fireworks have long been a part of **Independence** Day. They remind some people of war. Our country won its independence by fighting a war.

Independence is another way of saying "freedom." Why did our country have to win its freedom? From whom? That story begins about 400 years ago.

# Thirteen English Colonies

*Captain John Smith was the leader of Jamestown.*

Before the 1600s, few **Europeans** lived in North America. Then, a group of English people came to this land. In 1607, they built a village called Jamestown.

More **settlers** followed. They were **colonists.** They thought of themselves as English, but they lived here, far from their own country. Thirteen English **colonies** formed in North America.

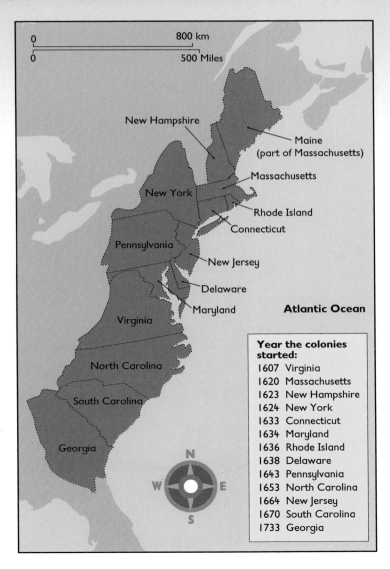

0 | 800 km
0 | 500 Miles

New Hampshire

Maine (part of Massachusetts)

Massachusetts

New York

Rhode Island

Connecticut

Pennsylvania

New Jersey

Delaware

Maryland

Atlantic Ocean

Virginia

North Carolina

South Carolina

Georgia

N W E S

**Year the colonies started:**
1607 Virginia
1620 Massachusetts
1623 New Hampshire
1624 New York
1633 Connecticut
1634 Maryland
1636 Rhode Island
1638 Delaware
1643 Pennsylvania
1653 North Carolina
1664 New Jersey
1670 South Carolina
1733 Georgia

9

# A Busy New World

The **colonists** did well in this new land. They grew **crops** and caught fish. They sawed trees into **lumber.**

What they could not make, they bought. They traded with one another and with England, too. New towns grew quickly in this land.

# Growing Apart

At first, the **colonists** were **loyal** to England and its king. But England was far away. When the colonists needed help, they could not get it from England.

So they took care of most problems on
their own. As time passed, they felt less and
less connected to England—or Great
Britain, as it was called after 1707.

★

# The French and Indian War

In 1754, Great Britain went to war with France. Part of this war was fought in North America. This part was called the French and Indian War.

*Many Native Americans fought on the side of the French during the French and Indian War.*

The **British** won the French and Indian
War. They forced the French out of North
America. But the war had cost a lot of
money. It left the British king in **debt.**

# The King's Taxes

The **British** king was George the Third. He decided to get money from the **colonists** in North America. He ordered them to pay him many new **taxes.**

The colonists thought these taxes were unfair. They had not **voted** for a war. The king's **debt** was not their fault. The money would not be spent on their needs.

# Angry Colonists

In fact, the **colonists** had no **vote** in the **British government.** So why should they pay British **taxes?** They asked this question to the king.

King George did not want to answer this question. He sent soldiers to keep the colonists quiet. The colonists were forced to let the soldiers live in their homes!

# Trouble in Boston

In 1770, trouble broke out in Boston. On March 5, **British** soldiers shot five **colonists** dead. People in the **colonies** were shocked. This was called the Boston **Massacre.**

*Patrick Henry (standing, left) gave a famous speech to a group of colonists on March 23, 1775.*

The colonists began to see Great Britain as an enemy. They spoke of breaking away from that country. "Give me **liberty** or give me death," cried a colonist leader named Patrick Henry.

# War Breaks Out

*Paul Revere warned the colonists that the British were coming.*

In 1775, a **British** general thought the **colonists** were planning to make trouble. He decided to take away their **gunpowder.** But the colonists knew he was coming.

Some colonists hid near the villages of Concord and Lexington in Massachusetts. When the British marched past, they started shooting. The Revolutionary War had begun.

# The Declaration of Independence

*Thomas Jefferson*

What exactly were the **colonists** fighting for? A man named Thomas Jefferson put it into words. His statement is called the **Declaration** of **Independence.**

Jefferson wrote that people have a right to choose their own leaders. He said the colonists no longer wanted **British** leaders or their laws. This announcement was signed on July 4, 1776.

*The Declaration of Independence was read to the public on July 8, 1776 in Philadelphia, Pennsylvania.*

# A Nation Is Born

King George refused to let the **colonies** go. He sent his armies to North America. But the **colonists** fought back. They were led by George Washington.

*British General Cornwallis (left) gave up to George Washington (center) in the last battle of the Revolutionary War.*

The Revolutionary War lasted eight years. In 1781, the **British** were beaten. The colonists could now form their own country. They formed the United States in 1783.

# Many People, One Country

Americans have come from many places. Our country has grown from 13 **colonies** to 50 states.

Together, we have built one country.
It belongs to no one except us **citizens.**
Fireworks on **Independence** Day help
us celebrate our freedom and pride in
our country.

# Important Dates

## Independence Day

| | |
|---|---|
| **1492** | Christopher Columbus first explores the Americas |
| **1607** | Jamestown is founded |
| **1733** | Georgia, the thirteenth **colony,** is founded |
| **1754** | French and Indian War begins |
| **1763** | French and Indian War ends |
| **1765** | The Stamp Act creates many new **taxes** for **colonists** |
| **1768** | **British** soldiers arrive in Boston, Massachusetts |
| **1770** | The Boston **Massacre** |
| **1775** | The Revolutionary War begins |
| **1776** | **Declaration** of **Independence** |
| **1781** | General Cornwallis surrenders at Yorktown |
| **1783** | The Revolutionary War ends |
| **1787** | The Constitution is written |
| **1789** | George Washington becomes the first president of the United States |

# Glossary

**British**  people from the country of Great Britain

**citizens**  members of a country

**colony**  group of people who live in a new land, but remain loyal to their home country

**colonists**  people who live in a colony

**crops**  plants grown by farmers for food and other uses

**debt**  owing someone money

**declaration**  statement that announces something

**Europeans**  people from the continent of Europe

**government**  all the people who govern a country, state, city, or town

**gunpowder**  exploding powder used to fire bullets

**independence**  being on one's own; not under someone else's control

**liberty**  freedom

**loyal**  faithful to; ready to serve and follow

**lumber**  wood sawed into boards

**massacre**  killing of many people who cannot fight back. The Boston Massacre was not a true massacre because only five people died.

**settlers**  people who move to a new place to live

**taxes**  money that a government collects from its citizens

**vote**  to make one's choice

# More Books to Read

Dalgliesh, Alice. *The 4th of July Story.* New York: Simon & Schuster Children's Publishing, 1995.

Kalman, Bobbie. *Holidays.* New York: Crabtree Publishing, 1997.

Landau, Elaine. *Independence Day.* Berkeley Heights, N.J.: Enslow Publishers, Inc., 2001.

# Index